W9-AUC-358

EXCUSES
EXCNSES

Which One
is Yours?

Living the Excuse Free Life

BY PETER LOPEZ, JR.

Excuses Excuses Which One is Yours?
Living the Excuse Free Life
by Peter Lopez, Jr.

Printed in the United States of America

ISBN 9781498401869

Scripture.quotations taken from the King James Version of the Bible, Public Domain.

www.xulonpress.com

I dedicate this book to my wife Sorines G. Lopez
My 3 sons
Peter Jacob Lopez
Jonathyn Andrew Lopez
Malachi Nick Lopez

Table of Contents

Introduction

We all have our beginnings. Some people begin their lives in a hospital room, others at home, while still others begin their lives in a small hut with hard packed earth covered in dirt for floors. Maybe you were born in the United States or maybe you were born in a third world country. A room may have been flooded with gifts from an elaborate baby shower or maybe you were wrapped with the same blanket that your five brothers before you were also wrapped in when they were born. Regardless of the specifics, they don't matter in the sense that we all have our beginnings. However, if you are close to giving birth, I certainly recommend that you do everything you can for your newborn because beginnings themselves are important, no matter the circumstances.

It is important to give thought and make plans for what matters when a life begins; being purposeful about the details can transcend the bigger picture and give a child a positive start. Beginnings are where we first learn sounds and feel moods. Although we don't know what the words mean, we experience the atmosphere around us and it becomes part of our human experience. It is where we are first fed our nourishment, either directly from our mother or a plastic bottle. Several years ago I birthed a four-week sermon series titled *Excuses-Excuses: We All Have Them — Which One is Yours?* I preached the series when I was a senior pastor in Milford, Massachusetts. Throughout my time in ministry, I kept coming back to these same notes time after time, whether it was another sermon or I was traveling to a different city or country to speak.

Little did I know that this series, from long ago, would become a book. My intent at the time was to challenge the church. I felt we had become complacent; we were way too comfortable. As the body of Christ, we were not experiencing the growth that is vital to a living organization. At some point however, things have to change because the fact of the matter is, God won't keep you in your comfort zone for too long. Unfortunately, we throw out excuse after excuse and delay His purpose. Excuses somehow make us feel good about not being as great as we can be. Like a hamster on a wheel, excuses keep us moving and at the same time keep us from getting anywhere. *It's important to remember that God will do whatever*

He has to do to guide you to His purpose for your life. God is calling people who are seeking, not sitting.

At the time that I preached the series, the church met the challenge I presented to them and it marked my life. Because of the effect it was having in the lives of our congregation, people began to ask, "What is being taught, preached and (more importantly) believed?" It was clear that God had not only placed this message in my heart, but also put me in a position where I was able to connect with other leaders and mentor them. The purpose here is not just to help you self-identify the ways that you have been using excuses, but more importantly to give you the tools and encouragement you need to take responsibility for what you have managed to avoid with those excuses.

P.E.S. — Programmed Excuse Syndrome

Whenever we want to get out of a situation we have always been able to find an excuse, right? Have you been in a situation when someone wanted you to do something, but you really didn't want to do it? That's when P.E.S. just takes its natural course and before you know it you blurted out an "excuse". You say, "Oh this Saturday? I'm booked already," when there's nothing on your calendar. Have you ever showed up late to a meeting, dinner, sales appointment, wedding or even your son's graduation? The first person that greets you gets the P.E.S. right away, don't they? "Wow, there was so much traffic on Route 95. I didn't think it would take me that long and when I looked at the gas gauge, I noticed I was almost empty."

"Oh, it started at 6:00 PM? I thought you said 7:00..." For those of us who are that good at it, we get people to give our excuses for us, right? "Hey, Jimmy's here; he thought dinner was at 7." We automatically go into the file in our heads, pull out a fitting excuse and insert it in the right place and time. Some of us plan our excuses in advance, while others can give an excuse to any situation at the drop of a hat. Which one are you?

"He that is good at making excuses is seldom good at anything else."
—Benjamin Franklin

Welcome to your first day of an excuse-free life. We are all programmed to throw out excuse after excuse and we don't think twice about it. I'm a living example of getting out of situations by using simple, everyday excuses. I have deflected blame by shielding myself with excuse after excuse.

Excuses are the softest little white lies. They feel so good coming out of your mouth and most of the time we don't realize we're saying them.

"Excuses change nothing, but make everyone feel better."
— Mason Cooley

The problem with excuses is that without realizing it, we allow them to shape our future. We don't realize it, but our families and those around us suffer because of our inability to be accountable. Your dreams will never leave your pillow, your weight will never decrease and your IQ will never go up. The worst thing is God's will for your life never gets accomplished.

I am going to tackle this extremely important subject in a lighthearted way. My prayer is that when you read this you can identify the Father of Lies in all of his subtlety and see the ruin that your excuses are causing you, your family and your calling.

"If you really want to do it, you do it. There are no excuses."
— Bruce Nauman

If you're like me you probably don't know who Bruce Nauman is, but he is a world-renowned sculptor, photographer and artist. He was voted as one of TIME Magazine's 100 Most Influential People in 2004. The point is, it's really that simple, so let's get started.

First things first, in order to live an excuse-free life, we need to understand what "excuse" really means. The Merriam-Webster Dictionary defines "excuse" as:

A. To make apology for

B. To try to remove blame from

Other definitions state: "An excuse is an attempt to lessen the blame attached to a fault." "To use an excuse is to seek to defend or justify an action or inaction." Here's my favorite: "A reason put forward to conceal the real reason for an action or inaction."

As I write this book today, I work for a book publishing company as a publishing consultant. People call in from all over the world; I'm the guy on the other end of the phone that listens to their ideas and takes the time to consult with them. I encourage them; I partner with them and help fulfill their dream of writing and publishing their book. It is the first time most of them ever really consider themselves as an author, which is a significant accomplishment. I have been in the trenches with hundreds of aspiring authors. I ask them what's holding them back. I even coined a phrase, "Two pages a day will get your book published right away." One day I realized God has been using me for over 20 years to share hope and motivation with multitudes of people, using words like, "Go and boldly live out your dreams." "Don't look back,

Excuses have been part of our makeup since the birth of man; they're evident throughout the Bible.

keep moving forward, you can do all things in Christ who strengthens you." "You have the seed of greatness" and so on and so forth.

I tell them their dream is literally in their hands and you know what? They respond! By the grace of God I have been able to help hundreds of Christian authors finish and publish their books! Do you know the crazy thing about being part of hundreds of books that will help people, bring about blessings to an untold amount of Gods people? I hadn't done it myself! The company I work for wanted me to write a book. They would even publish it for me. Still, I hadn't written one. I'm not a good typist, so I bought software that types perfectly what I speak and I still hadn't started. Would you like to know why I hadn't written a book? *Excuses*. I guess we get them for free at the Excuse Academy or something.

We wake up every day wanting to lose weight, wanting to exercise, wanting to open a business, wanting to go back to school, wanting to spend more time with our families, or wanting to (insert your personalized "want" here). We've prayed about it, dreamed about it and some of us have driven people completely nuts because we don't stop talking about it! At the end of the day though… where is it? *We are still in the same place!* You don't like the fact that you can't go out to eat when you want to because you live paycheck to paycheck and only on your second monthly paycheck can you afford to go to a restaurant. However, going to school to get a better job is going to take two to four years! You don't have that kind of time, right? Fast-forward to five years later and *you still don't like the fact that you can't go out to eat when you want to* because you still live paycheck to paycheck, but you still don't have time to go back to school. Really?

Your desire is to travel the world, but you still haven't even gotten your passport! Your desire is to (insert desire here) but you still haven't (insert what you should've done already here)! Do you know why? I do. You have been making excuses! I'll repeat what I said earlier because it's important. *Excuses somehow make you feel good about not being as great as you can be.* I don't know about you, but I got sick and tired of how my excuses kept holding me back. Twenty years went by and there was still no book thanks to excuses like: "I don't have the time to sit and write and when I do, how do I begin the book." "I'm too busy being busy" and so on. Being sick and tired will not remove your excuses, but you have to get sick and tired and do something about it!

I finally got to that point and declared, "I was going to try to live an excuse-free life" and this book became a reality—you're holding it! If you're sick and tired of the excuses that keep you from reaching your next level, I truly believe you're reading the right book for this season.

There *are* no excuses!

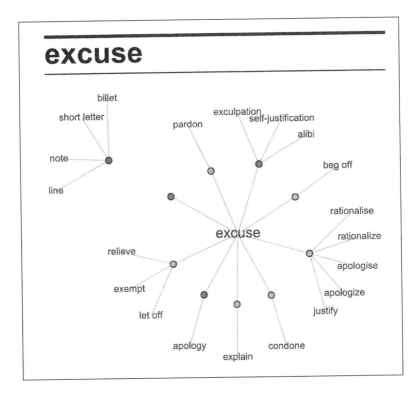

Images from the Visual Thesaurus, http://www.visualtheasaurus.com, Copyright © 2014 Thinkmap, Inc. All rights reserved.

PART I

The Problem

Chapter 1

The Excuse of Family

———◦❧◦———

If you're married, you've probably used your spouse to get out of so many things. It's so easy to say, "I would like to, but my husband…" or "I would, but you see, my wife…" Don't act like you haven't done it. I know I've done it. Have you ever had to inform your spouse of your excuse so he or she can cover for you, too? It goes something like this: "If Martha asks what we're doing on Saturday, tell her the same excuse I told her." You're smiling right now because you've been there. Let me translate this for you. The context of this conversation is actually: "Martha wants me to go to her house for her latest MLM party idea and I'm really not interested in going, so I lied to her. You know how Martha is. She'll probably ask you, so now you have to lie to her, too. Otherwise, it will look like I lied to her."

Now, being the good spouse that you have, he or she needs to lie to poor Martha as well. Oh wait. It's not a lie; it's an excuse. "The man said, 'The woman you put here with me—she gave me some fruit from the tree, and I ate it" (Genesis 3:12). Let's put this in its proper context. God created Adam and Adam knew it. Adam didn't think that the monkey he named "monkey" was in some way a part of his existence other than that they shared the same Creator. Adam knew God created him because God told him—in person! God created Adam and told him that the earth was his dominion. All that he saw was his to name as he saw fit. God had created the perfect place for man, a place where Adam could really be himself.

You know that feeling, don't you? No one is in the house and you get out of the shower and decide not to put on your robe because you're home alone and oh so comfortable. That's exactly the kind of place that God gave to Adam and like us, he didn't bother putting on a robe. He might've even done some really embarrassing singing and dancing, too, like us when we're home alone! The great thing about being home alone is you're alone. The bad thing about being home alone though is… you're alone. After too long, you crave company. Sometimes you will settle for anyone's company, which is how people get in bad relationships, but that's another topic for another day.

Can you imagine the kind of conversations God and Adam shared? As days went by, give or take a thousand years, Adam realized there were different types of creatures, male and female, but only one of him. There were none like him, so God said, "It's not good for man to be alone" and instead of creating another like him, He created another unique being to be his companion. He created woman, Eve. *"The woman you gave me…"* God gave Adam everything, including a rule. "Do not eat of that tree." Sure enough, the man that has everything takes the one thing he can't have. That fruit from that tree.

> Then the man and his wife heard the sound of the Lord God as he was walking in the garden in the cool of the day, and they hid from the Lord God among the trees of the garden. But the Lord God called to the man, "Where are you?" He answered, "I heard you in the garden, and I was afraid because I was naked; so I hid." And he said, "Who told you that you were naked? Have you eaten from the tree that I commanded you not to eat from?" The man said, "The woman you put here with me—she gave me some fruit from the tree, and I ate it." Then the

Lord God said to the woman, "What is this you have done?" The woman said, "The serpent deceived me, and I ate." (Genesis 3:8-13)

Pause—of course God knew he ate from the tree, but sometimes it's better to ask a question than to accuse, isn't it? Adam had a choice. Do I accept the blame or "excuse" myself? If you know the story, you know he resorted to giving an excuse rather than accepting full responsibility for his actions. I get it. I've been there. If an excuse were a boxer, it would be the Pound for Pound Champion. Adam resorted to deflecting; he resorted to blaming... he resorted to using an excuse!

Adam resorted to making an excuse.

Can we talk for a sec... you and me? Yes, you. Let us reason together for a moment, shall we? There are excuses and there are reasons. There is a difference between the two—a big difference. Webster's Dictionary has about 18 different definitions for the word "reason" and here's one of them: To bring (someone) to reason, to induce a change of opinion in (someone) through presentation of arguments; convince. e.g. "The mother tried to bring her rebellious daughter to reason." By reason of, on account of;

because of; e.g. "He was consulted about the problem by reason of his long experience." You are able to justify a reason by giving a true account; excuses are seldom true, therefore they have no justification. I have three sons who try to reason with me all the time in many different ways. I have tried to use that same "reasoning" on my wife, when things don't go my way, which seldom happens. (Now let's not forget, it's you and me talking here.)

"The woman *you* put here with me — she gave me some fruit from the tree, and I ate it." Is Adam really trying to blame God here? Oh, yes he is! Can you believe the audacity of that man? I bet you can. It's because of our own actions that we had to invent words like "audacity" in the first place. Look, Adam, I get it. You felt bad. God had done so much for you and you let him down. I'm telling you, I get it. I get it when you use your excuse. If you didn't feel bad, you wouldn't feel the need to invent something, to put your reputation on the line so the other person doesn't take offense to your late arrival or no-show. "And the woman said, 'The serpent deceived me, I did eat'" (Genesis 3:13). Eve, mother of all living things, are you really telling God it's not your fault, either? It's that serpent's fault... the one that God allowed in the Garden. So... it's really God's fault?

The Excuses We Use

1. "I wasn't born with a silver spoon in my mouth."
   Translation: I am not going to act proper because it's easier for me to behave this way and I'll just blame it on my parents for not making enough money. Because my parents didn't make enough money, it absolves me of acting with a certain level of class or decorum.

2. "It's not just me; no one in my family has gone to college and I mean *no one!*"
   Translation: Look, I'm scared. What if I start and don't finish? Worse, what if I start and I fail my classes? How am I going to explain that? I know it's been on my mind lately and I really do want to provide more for my family, but I'm just not that brave.

3. "Do you know where I'm from?"
   Translation: I'm embarrassed, but let me deflect this embarrassment from myself and blame it on society. Maybe if I can make them feel bad because I was born in a bad part of town, I'll be excused from my latest indiscretion.

News Flash Those excuses don't work. They don't absolve you from whatever you're trying to get out of. In fact, all they do is make you look bad or worse, a liar! Let's get back to the story and I'll show you how this works. God is being handed excuses from Adam and Eve. Neither one has the guts to say, "God, I'm sorry. I fell in a moment of weakness and I ate from that tree; please forgive me." Instead they played the blame game, thinking it would make them blameless. They didn't make themselves accountable and because they didn't, God held them accountable. To the woman He said, "I will make your pains in childbearing very severe; with painful labor you will give birth to children. Your desire will be for your husband, and he will rule over you."

The serpent deceived you? Are you kidding me? Since when have you paid attention to the serpent? And why did you give it to Adam? Did the serpent also tell you to give it to Adam? I don't believe your excuse Eve; I know all. I would have forgiven you had you admitted your disobedience, but instead you chose excuses. To the man He said, "Cursed is the ground because of you; through painful toil, you will eat food from it all the days of your life. It will produce thorns and thistles for you and you will eat the plants of the field. By the sweat of your brow you will eat your food until you return to the ground, since from it you were taken; from dust you are and to dust you will return."

Translation: Wow! I thought we were cool! When Eve came to you with the fruit, why didn't you tell her you weren't going to eat it? Why didn't you tell her you and I have talked for ages and although you're curious, you knew it wasn't the right thing to do? I gave her to you as your companion and now you're telling me whenever she offers you something you are helpless to say no? Hmmm... nope, I just don't believe it. Now everything is about to change. No more free meals. No more everything being handed to you; now you have to work the land. Last, but certainly not least, because you chose to give me an excuse, you are going to go back to the dust from where I brought you.

Excuses are the death of us!

Let me sum this up to those of you who don't think it's not a big deal to give excuses. It is because of excuses that women have labor during childbirth and it is the reason why we live mortal lives! Simply put, excuses are the death of us!

You might be thinking, "Whoa, whoa—wait a minute! I thought this was a light-hearted book that will empower me to be all I can be. What's with all this death talk?" Let me make this clear—this is a light-hearted book. If you practice the tools, you will learn from this book it will lighten your heart. The reason for the death talk is that this is what your excuses are doing to you. Your excuses are killing your potential.

26

Your excuses are killing your dreams. Your excuses are killing your marriage. Your excuses are killing your career. Your excuses are killing your relationships.

It is time for you to stop making excuses for yourself. It's not working for you. Excuses are your enemy. Read that aloud: "Excuses are my enemy."

I would do more in my church, but my church (*add your excuse here*).

Church? Let me tell you why I don't go to church…
Why do I only go to church on Sunday? Let me tell you about my church…
Why am I not more involved at my church? Let me tell you…
Why don't I give offering or tithe at my church? Let me tell you…
Why don't I invite anyone to my church? Let me tell you…

What would you like to hear? Would you like me to say that because your church is not full of perfect people, you shouldn't follow the biblical principles of gathering at a church? I can't write that. See, my keyboard will blow up if I type those words. How's that for a dumb excuse? Guess what? It's just as dumb as your excuses. *News Flash* Church leaders aren't perfect people. Shocked? Stop it. If your church isn't perfect, but striving for perfection, you're at the right place. If your church is biblically sound, you're at the right place. If there are imperfect people at your church, you're at the right place.

Stop making excuses for why you're not doing what is in your heart. Stop blaming others and start looking at yourself. Examine your life. In mere seconds you will identify what is holding you back from living up to God's purpose for your life. Take a moment and grab a pen and paper. I'll wait here for you to get back. Promise. OK. You got the pen and paper? I was serious! Go ahead and grab a pen and paper! Title the page: *My Lame Excuses for Not Serving My Full Potential.* Now start making your list. It's okay if you only have one excuse, but you have to admit to at least have one. We are going to close this chapter and you will have a piece of paper with your excuses. Now pay attention, this is important. I want you to pray over that piece of paper. In your prayer, tell God that you know that somehow you believed that lie. Tell God that you are His and are willing to do what it takes to live an excuse-free life.

Now blow that paper up or pin it on your mirror and laugh out loud when you read it, because you're dropping out of the Excuse Academy and you can't believe you used such excuses like the one on your page. You are royalty. You are a child of the King of Kings. You come from the line of David, that same David who killed Goliath, that same David who danced for the Lord in the street! Once you received the Lord Jesus as your personal Lord and Savior, your family has changed. No longer do you come from that alcoholic family. No longer do you come from a family without means. No longer do you come from a family of nobodies. Your family is no longer a reason that you need an excuse for. Your family is your strength.

Chapter 2

The Excuse of Yourself

"And Moses said unto Jehovah, 'Oh Lord, I am not eloquent, neither heretofore, nor since thou hast spoken unto thy servant; for I am slow of speech, and of a slow tongue'" (Exodus 4:10). In chapter one we read about how we blame our families, our upbringing or where we come from. However, in this chapter we are going to look within; what do we do when we are our excuse? It's easier to blame someone else other than ourselves and deflect the blame. For those of you who are honest enough to accept some blame, I commend you. Good stuff. You are closer than the "it's not my fault" people. You have identified the enemy. Your enemy is you! The fact is that often we are our greatest enemies, our worst critics. We feed ourselves insecurity over and over again. The problem with that is that no matter how often you feed yourself with insecurity, you will never get full. You will never reach your potential.

Moses starts with "Oh, Lord." We can replace the old-school word "oh" with the new school word "but". You know the word; you've used it thousands of times before.

"But what was I supposed to do?"
"But I get so busy."
"But that's not my calling."
"But I'm not heading up the men's ministry."
"But the pastor didn't ask me to."
"But I'm broke. But I'm too short. But I don't have a degree."
"But I'm a single mom. But it's not the right time."

But this. But that.

When you use the word "but" it cancels whatever you are about to say next. Pay attention to this; write it down somewhere. *Your excuses will cancel your destiny before you are able to live it!* "But Lord, I don't speak well enough to even talk to the people and you want me to talk in front of royalty at the palace?"

The crazy thing about this excuse from Moses is that he is talking one on one with God here! I mean, when you are in a conversation with the Almighty where you can audibly hear his voice and you're conversing with him in real time—how do you put up an excuse? That is the moment you just say, "OK, you got it Jehovah, I'll do it." *What we need to understand is that once we rely on using excuses as a way out, they take a life of their own.* Moses lived with excuses all his life. Yeah, he lived in the palace as a prince, *but* he was still an Israelite so he was never a real prince. Yeah, he was an Israelite, *but* he lived in a palace like a prince so he wasn't a real Israelite. He grew up with so many excuses about this and that he had several excuses programmed and ready to use when he spoke with the Lord of Hosts.

Can you believe that the "I don't speak well" excuse wasn't even his first one? When God told him that he wanted him to speak to His people, the first thing Moses said was, "What if they don't believe me?"

◄———— *Ex* ————►

When you use the word "but" it cancels whatever you are about to say next.

◄———— *Ex* ————►

God asked Moses, "What do you have in your hand?" Moses answered, "A staff."

God said, "Throw it down on the ground."

Moses threw it on the ground so that it became a snake and Moses ran from it. *He ran from it. Moses ran from the miracle that God had just performed.* Someone reading this right now has seen God at work, yet they are running from their calling. You have thanked

God for this and you have thanked God for that. You acknowledge the miracle that He has performed in your own life; how He has changed you, how He has transformed your family life yet you are running from your destiny. God tells you right now to reach out and grab that snake by the tail. Don't be scared of it. It's the enemy who needs to be scared of it. The world needs people bold enough to call a miracle a miracle, embrace the supernatural manifestations and step into their calling.

Moses grabbed the snake by its tail and it turned into a staff once again, yet he still wasn't convinced. God had to show him yet another miracle. "Put your hand inside your cloak," He said. When Moses took his hand out, it was leprous! God told Moses to put his hand back in his cloak again and when he took it out, it was restored. God saw into Moses's heart and knew that Moses still wasn't convinced! God said, "If they don't pay attention to both signs, take some water from the Nile and pour it on the ground and I will turn the water into blood." It was after all that when Moses threw out the excuse of his inability to speak well.

This book was not written to beat you up for making excuses. This book exists to tell you that even the greatest of us threw out excuses at one point or another. What I want to tell you is that the day has come for you to examine yourself—call an excuse an excuse and stop believing the lies you surround your-self with on why you can't live up to your potential. God's answer to Moses was that it is Him who gave us a mouth. It is Him who makes people deaf or mute. It's interesting that Jesus would say to a multitude of people with perfectly good hearing "Those who can hear, hear this." See? It is God who allows our words to connect with the heart, not our ability. God said, "Who makes the deaf or mute? Who gives them sight or makes them blind? Is it not I, the Lord?" Look at that in the supernatural. "Who makes them deaf or mute, who gives them sight or makes them blind?"

God simply steamrolled all over Moses's excuses. Do you know why? Because they don't actually matter. In your mind, excuses have the power to redirect you from a certain direction at a certain time, *but in no way do they change God's plan for your life.* God isn't telling someone else to do it; He put it in *your* heart for *you* to do it. Open your mouth. Lead them. Start that business. Start that life group. Fill out that school application. You know that family is struggling; give them that love offering. When the excuses are gone, what reason do you have left on why not to do it? None. So do it.

Back to the story: God tells Moses to use Aaron to help him speak. The wonderful part of it all is that it ends up being Moses who tells the Pharaoh, "Let my people go." Once you embark on God's plan in your life, God may bring people to help you along the way, but at the end of the day it will be you who fulfilled that calling because that calling is yours. When God leads you in a direction, when God calls you to do something, what he is looking for is not necessarily the outcome, but your obedience. Too many people fear the outcome so much that they don't obey. God never told Moses that it was his job to convince anyone of anything. God will do the convincing; all you have to do is talk. It is God who changes the heart. It is God who changes the atmosphere. It is God who changes the situations.

It is God who does the miracle. What he wants you to do is something you are fully capable of doing. Don't fear the outcome. Don't fear failure. Don't fear the possibility that no one will come or no one will care. Don't fear what people will say. Step into your destiny—fulfill God's plan in your life and He will take care of the outcome! This world is full of "Oh Lord" people. If Moses had stayed an "Oh Lord" guy, the nation of Israel would never have been freed. We would never have heard of him. What about you? Who is going to hear about you?

Chapter 3

The Excuse of The People

"Do not be angry, my lord," Aaron answered. "You know how prone these people are to evil" (Exodus 32:22). Now it gets juicy. In this chapter we aren't going to talk about your family or even you. We are going to talk about other people: friends, acquaintances and strangers. The people! In my early years of being a leader, it was difficult for me to go against The People. On a certain occasion Deacon Bob came up to me one time and confided to me that The People weren't too happy with some of the changes I implemented. Before I was a Pastor, The People saw me as someone they could confide in and would tell me things they wouldn't tell others. Naturally, I assumed when my trusted Deacon Bob would tell me The People didn't like the changes I implemented, I thought that a lot of different people had come to him as they once used to come up to me with their concerns.

It took a while for me to figure out that when Deacon Bob said, "The People" he was referring to his unhappy wife Roberta, who hated the church and his cousin Robert, who disliked my style of preaching! I am not proud as I admit to you that while I was the Pastor of a church that was growing a mature and thriving congregation, I made decisions based on five unhappy people. As a leader or a person of influence, you are faced with decisions all of the time. On many occasions you will have a strong conviction about topics, procedures and philosophies. However, there are also many times when you lean on your staff and their talents. You do everything in your power to do the will of God. You are tasked with being a shepherd to The People.

The problem arises when you try to please The People. Beware of the rabbit hole of pleasing The People; it goes nowhere. Please God and The People will follow. Aaron wasn't just anyone at the time he asked Moses not to be angry with him. He was The High Priest, The Big Dog. Moses came to Aaron first and Aaron saw the miracles God performed. Moses was away talking to God and Aaron was in charge. The People complained to him that Moses was gone and they needed a God they could look at, being that they didn't know when or if Moses would be back. We will never know how many of The People were part of those who complained to Aaron. Maybe it was 80%! Maybe it was 20%. Maybe it was just five really loud, really unhappy people.

He didn't put something in your heart and your mind for you to run it by so and so for their blessing. I have yet to find some place in the Bible where God tells a person to do something, but before he does, maybe he should ask his best friend if she thinks it's a good idea. If you find it in the Bible, let me know. I have a couple of them fancy degrees on theology and Bible stuff, but hey, I could be wrong. Then again, I could be right about this: God doesn't call The People. God calls individuals to lead The People! Sure, God will give a church a purpose, but that's a totally different topic. He calls on leaders to lead. When you start trying to hear the voices of The People over the voice of God, that's when trouble comes. Lead The People, care for The People, love The People, but don't worry about the people. They will either follow you or go somewhere else. Your job is to do the job God gave you.

Let me tell you this: for your calling, God didn't call The People—He called You.

Some of you may be thinking that I'm a renegade and that I've never submitted; that I always danced to the beat of a different drum. That couldn't be further from the truth. I served under different ministries. I've served as a layperson, an assistant, an armor bearer and a gopher. The point is that I never would have accomplished half the things in my life that God has allowed me to do if I had ever given more sway to the voices of The People than to the voice of God. Moses got so angry when he saw what the people were doing that he broke incredibly special tablets he was bringing to the people. "The tablets were the work of God; the writing was the writing of God, engraved on the tablets" (Exodus 32:16).

God's handwriting, folks! Moses threw the tablets and broke them at the foot of the mountain. *Pay attention to this: within moments you can destroy what God said to you by listening to The People!* That's how quick it can happen. One moment you're listening to The People and looking at a Golden Calf and the next moment something precious, something uniquely given to you by God can slip from your hands. Do you want to know who The People care about? OK, I'll tell you. The People care about The People. This is one of the saddest events of the Bible because it speaks of utter selfishness of people who had been liberated from the yolk of slavery! *These people walked across dry ground and looked up at the walls of water when God parted the Red Sea. Years later they were asking for another God.* It was because of The People that Moses and Aaron never entered into The Promised Land! Are you getting this?

Let me see if I can make this clearer for you with a simple question. God has done miracles in your life, but you are going to cower before The People? Look at how it worked out for Aaron. Trust me when I tell you that you will never fulfill God's plan for your life when you care more about what The People say than what He says. Whether or not they listen to you should in no way decide whether you listen to Him. Before you take this out of context, I'm not saying you shouldn't trust mentors or pastors or talk things over with your spouse. There is that saying that goes: "You can't pick your family, but you can pick your friends." Have you heard it? It's a true saying. You choose your friends. Slow down and read that again. *You* choose *your* friends.

Anyone not related to you through blood is in your life because you have chosen him or her. Remember that the next time your "friend" doesn't act like a true friend. You choose your mentors, your pastors and your spouse. I'm not saying you should disregard the opinion of someone God has chosen to help you. Just don't listen to the loudness of the crowd and miss the whisper of His voice. The excuse of The People is telling of a weak-minded, weak-willed and insecure person. This excuse will drown out the great voice in your life — His.

Chapter 4

The Excuse of Your Past

"Pardon me, my lord," Gideon replied, "but how can I save Israel? My clan is the weakest in Manasseh, and I am the least in my family" (Judges 6:15). OK, you're at Chapter 4 with me. Awesome! It appears you are embarking on living an excuse-free life. Just imagine that for a moment: an excuse-free life! Is such a thing even possible? It is. When you live a life of integrity and honor, it is. When you walk by faith and not by sight, it definitely is. Before we get into the story of Gideon, let me share with you a little more about me, because in this chapter I'm going to ask you to look at your past. We all have a past, a history. Some are proud of their pasts, while it brings others shame. You are going to take one final look at your past and never look back again.

Why take one more look, you ask? I'll tell you why—for your testimony! Those of you that are happy with your history are more fortunate than I was. You can channel those early years as springboards to hurdle a lot of obstacles that life throws at us.

Turn a bad past into a good future.

I grew up in the slums of the Bronx, the South Bronx. Crime was on the menu every day. My family lived on food stamps and free cheese. I personally stood in the free cheese lines for hours. I heard more Spanish than English and just about everyone I grew up with did, too. Some people came into this country speaking more English than I did. It seemed like drugs were seen more on an everyday basis than hot water. I had every excuse not to succeed, except that my father, the great Reverend Pedro Lopez, Sr., would teach us a very important lesson in those days. Being poor and acting poor are two different things. I suffered racism, poverty, horrible teachers, the South Bronx projects, crime, and just about everything the world could throw at me.

I have known people who were much more gifted than me succumb to using excuses and go nowhere. I have seen wonderful people fall in love with their excuses only to be betrayed by them time and time again. I couldn't allow myself to be like them. I knew that one day I would have a wife and children and I didn't want to tell them that we live in poverty because of (insert excuse after excuse). I learned early on that excuses are a form of poison. They paralyze you with false reasoning and you fail to act. You substitute excuses in the place of what needs to be done. Since then I have put myself through school, traveled these great United States and been to over 17 different countries. I married a beau-tiful woman from a famous band. I have owned and lived the American dream; sat with kings of nations, Supreme

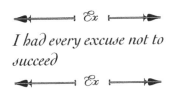

I had every excuse not to succeed

Court judges, high level politicians what some might call important people. Yada, yada, yada.

Check out what I've learned: *holding on to excuses is what keeps your past in front of you and not behind you.* Some of us still cling to the excuse of our pasts, allowing the past to shape who we are today and who we will be tomorrow. Turn your back on your past, whether it was good or bad. I know it's impossible to truly forget your past. Only God truly forgets our pasts; we can't. The fact that you can't forget it doesn't mean you have to carry it in your pocket and insert it into your mouth every time life challenges you. This book may not make the New York Times Bestseller List. Oprah might not make it the book of the month for her book club. *Sure, I think of those things as I write this, but what does that have to do with me writing it?*

If those were my goals in writing a book, I might never finish it. My goals for writing this book are to share what God put in my heart from His word and my experiences to get your limbs moving in the direction that He has pointed you to.

Activity Time

I want to ask for your permission for us to have a deeper connection than just the author/reader level. I would like to stand alongside you and walk with you for a while. What I would like is for you to grab a pen and a piece of paper and think about where you feel God is leading you. God likes his people seeking, not sitting—remember that. Now take that pen and write down the excuses you have allowed to stall you. It should look something like this:

1. My excuse for not writing a book is I'm not a good writer.
2. My excuse for not writing a book is I'm not per-fect. Who am I to give advice?
3. My excuse for not writing a book is I'm not sure what to write about.

4. My excuse for not writing a book is my closest friends think it would be a flop.

5. My excuse for not writing a book is I don't have the time.

6. My excuse for not writing a book is I don't have the money.

7. My excuse for not writing a book is I can't do this alone.

8. My excuse for not writing a book is I've never done anything like this before.

Did you write out your excuses? They might just be two, or even one, but that's ok. Don't underestimate the power of writing something down. The reason I want you to write it down is so that you don't forget them because next I want you to read them aloud. It is with our mouths that we confess and we are saved. OK, read them. Just once; don't get all excited and read them 20 times, once is enough. OK, did you say them? (Some of you have just continued to read this book without actually stopping to do what I'm asking you to do. I strongly urge you to do this exercise; it will definitely help you. What excuse could possibly be good enough for you not to do something that will help you?) Do it. Do it now.

OK, now you are going to take your list and at the end of each excuse you are going to write this: "...but

I serve an Awesome God, so that won't stop me." So now your list should look like this:

1. My excuse for not writing a book is I'm not a good writer, BUT I SERVE AN AWESOME GOD, SO THAT WON'T STOP ME!

2. My excuse for not writing a book is I'm not perfect, BUT I SERVE AN AWESOME GOD, SO THAT WON'T STOP ME!

3. My excuse for not writing a book is I'm not sure what to write about, BUT I SERVE AN AWESOME GOD, SO THAT WON'T STOP ME!

4. My excuse for not writing a book is my closest friends think it would be a flop, BUT I SERVE AN AWESOME GOD, SO THAT WON'T STOP ME!

5. My excuse for not writing a book is I don't have the time, BUT I SERVE AN AWESOME GOD, SO THAT WON'T STOP ME!

6. My excuse for not writing a book is I don't have the money, BUT I SERVE AN AWESOME GOD, SO THAT WON'T STOP ME!

7. My excuse for not writing a book is I can't do this alone, BUT I SERVE AN AWESOME GOD, SO THAT WON'T STOP ME!

8. My excuse for not writing a book is I've never done anything like this before, BUT I SERVE AN AWESOME GOD, SO THAT WON'T STOP ME!

Now read it aloud with conviction. Felt good right? Read it again. Align your spirit with this declaration. Feel the boldness of the Almighty. You are more than a conqueror. I didn't want to go all "motivational speaker" on you, but it's better to be cheesy than to keep doing what you've done thus far that has taken you nowhere. Before this book was written I wasted more than 20 years through using excuses. I first got the bug to write a book when I read one of those cool little Kenneth Hagin booklets my father had on his nightstand. Year after year, month after month, week after week, day after day I would tell myself, "This is the year to write and publish my book." Not bad, give and take the 87,600 days in between.

The Story

"Pardon me, my lord," Gideon replied, "but how can I save Israel? My clan is the weakest in Manasseh, and I am the least in my family" (Judges 6:15). OK, you know the drill. We are going to exchange "Pardon me, my lord" for "...but God." "But God, my family doesn't come from much and I'm the black sheep! I'm the screw up. I'm not the overachiever. I'm more of the class clown and not the class president. People don't tend to take me too seriously." It's interesting to note that Gideon is talking to an Angel of the Lord who just addressed him as a Mighty Warrior. Gideon wasn't just a mighty warrior with a great name, but he was also a Judge and in that time that's the closest thing they had to Kings. The first thing this warrior/judge/king says when God tells him that He will use him to save Israel is: "My clan is the weakest and I'm the least in my family."

I'm looking at this like, you have a clan? *How cool is that?!* He's looking at it as if someone should save Israel—just not him. *News Flash* Your family is Israel. Your community is Israel. Your church is Israel. Your future is Israel. God is calling you to save Israel. How are you responding? Before you distance yourself from our friend Gideon, think about the reasons you are not doing what you can to better your family. Why aren't you a part of your community? Why aren't you more involved in your church or business? Why aren't you taking steps to ensure a better future? Back to Gideon, he is there saying, "Look, Mr. Angel, I'm loving the white wings and I'll never figure out how that halo keeps perfectly balanced on your head, but there are more important people here than me. Have you talked to Mike or Bill or Bob or Marsha? Yeah, go talk to Marsha; she's a bulldog!"

His response is something like our modern-day, "Hey, I might be able to throw in a small charitable contribution with my next paycheck, but that's about all I can do to help." Have you read Judges 6? It might want to make you just shake Gideon up when you realize that even after speaking with an angel, he needs to see a sign from God! Not just one sign, he asks for a bunch of signs! I'm sorry, but I'm fed up with those "Lord give me a sign" people! "Lord give me a sign" is one of the greatest excuses in the church today. Below are bits of real conversations I've had with people that have driven me crazy:

Me: "So, when are you going to start the life group at your house that you told me God put in your heart? I gave you all the information you asked me for last month. Is there anything else you need?"
Him: "I asked God for a sign and I'm still waiting for it."
Me: "Really?!"

Me: "Hey, I haven't seen you in five years. How is that business you were about to start? You were so excited about it."

Him: "I want to make sure that it's God's will so I asked Him for a sign and I'm still waiting to wake up and the sun is not shining. As soon as it doesn't though, there is nothing holding me back. I'm so excited!"

Me: "The sun not to shine, huh? Wow!"

Come on!

My pastor used to tell this story. A man was in the ocean and prayed for God to save him. A boat came by and the good folks in the boat threw him a life preserver. "No thanks," he said. "God is going to save me!" A little while after the boat left, a helicopter arrived and a rescue crew dropped a ladder for him to climb. The man waived them off. "No thanks. God is going to save me!" The man eventually drowns and goes to heaven and says to God, "I asked you to save me, but you didn't! Why not?" God said to him, "Well I sent you a boat and a helicopter…" Here's my point with this: some of you are "waiting for a sign" from God. You're waiting for a miracle. What you don't understand is that He came into your life and transformed you. He took your pain and turned it into joy. He took your crying and turned into dancing. You're waiting for a miracle, but what you don't realize is that you are the miracle! You are the miracle! *You are the sign!*

I'm fed up with those "Lord, give me a sign" people. I'm also getting a little tired with those "Let me pray about it" people! Oh yeah, I said it, I literally know someone who has been praying for something for 11 years. You read that right: 11 years. You are still praying about it? Please take this to heart: if you're still praying about a direction to go in and you feel as if you have been praying for it way too long — He already answered you. The answer is no. The answer is that He has something else in mind for you. Move on. *God wants you moving, not sitting.* As I mentioned earlier, I work mostly with Christian authors. They call in and say God called them to write a book. We talk about their book, we plan it out, we work it into their budget, and we assign them editors, ghostwriters, account managers who give them different ideas on a number of things.

They say that they never thought they would get so much support and how great it all is... then they say, "I just need to pray about it." In my head I think, "Didn't you *just* start the conversation saying God called you to write a book? Now you see it's more possible than you thought before and now... you have to pray to the same God who called you?" That lame excuse is the one that cost me 20 years. Twenty whole years. There is a fear inside of you that has you crippled and your decision is to throw out the stall excuse of "Let me pray about it." Tell me you're scared. Tell me you're worried that your work might get criticized and it would hurt your feelings. I'll help you pray about that fear all day. Just rid yourself of those excuses.

Don't misunderstand me. In no way am I saying that you shouldn't pray about what's in your heart. Pray about everything. Do yourself the favor and pray. Pray—but then act! Make a decision. Don't let the enemy fool you to thinking you should ask God for a sign or you should keep praying about something that God already put in your heart to do. Let's get back to Gideon. God called Gideon and he threw out excuse after excuse. He needed to see sign after sign. Gideon thought he was the least influential person in his family and that his family was the least influential family. Still, all of Israel rallied to Gideon's call! In fact, too many people answered Gideon's call.

The Israelites were being pillaged on a regular basis. They were fed up and wanted to do something about it. What they needed was a leader! They needed someone to stand up. There are people today who are seeking for the truth. There is just so much information out there today and they want to know the truth; they want to live a life with love, peace, forgiveness, mercy and joy. They just need someone to stand up and tell them, "Jesus is the answer!" All of Israel responded to our boy Gideon, so much so that Gideon had to let most of them go! He let tens of thousands go back to their homes and stayed with just 300 men. God used those 300 men and performed a miracle. Israel annihilated their enemy. Gideon became a hero.

In the end, they asked the least influential of the weakest clan to be their King. Gideon turned them down and pointed them to the King of Kings. Do what God puts in your heart to do. Make sure to give Him the glory.

Your Past Is Past

I get it. You've been hurt. You've been lied to. You feel cheated. You've been abused. You've been mistreated. Some situations just weren't fair. You've been criticized. You've been kicked when you were down. You've been stabbed in the back. You're still hurting and I'm sorry for every bad thing that has happened to you. You know what else though? You've been redeemed! You've been sanctified! You've been found! Your feet have been put on solid ground! You've been given the great comforter. You've been touched by The Way, The Truth and The Life! Stop speaking to your past—it won't respond and all you are doing is wasting time. Look to fix your present course and your future will respond!

Chapter 5

The Excuse of "This Just Doesn't Make Sense"

———⟋✦⟍———

But Naaman went away angry and said, "I thought that he would surely come out to me and stand and call on the name of the Lord his God, wave his hand over the spot and cure me of my leprosy. Are not Abana and Pharpar, the rivers of Damascus, better than all the waters of Israel? Couldn't I wash in them and be cleansed?" So he turned and went off in a rage. (2 Kings 5:11, 12)

This just doesn't make sense!

My, what an awesome God we serve. We love to preach about our awesome God, don't we? There are a few wonderful songs of worship that talk about our God being an awesome God and we love to sing them, don't we? We love to because we believe it. It's true. We believe it in every fiber of our being. Our God is an Awesome God! Sometimes though, I don't get Him. I know I have a calling for X, so why are doors opening up for me in Y? I know I'm called to work with men, so why did the Pastor just call me to talk about the youth? They know I have a degree in Finance; why did they even bring up the open sales job?

"Lord, why is your will different than what I think it should be?" Have you ever thought that? Oh come on, be honest with yourself. Have you ever wanted something so bad, but for some reason another opportunity opened up instead? I was speaking with an author recently. She is a Pastor and a great writer and speaker. She told me that she never thought she would be speaking for a living as she shared with me her trials during her extensive years of education to obtain her doctorate. She joked that if she knew she would end up being a Pastor, she never would have spent so much time, energy, and money on her schooling. As I heard the rest of her story, I pointed out to her that she was on the path that God wanted for her all along.

See, it was through one of the relationships she had forged during her years as a student that first opened the door for her to start preaching. Today she gives conferences and is flown all over the country to preach the word of God; she blesses people with the words that come out of her mouth, not her degree. However, if she were never on the path to get that degree, she would have never met the person that gave her the opportunity to start preaching! Often our problem is that we think there should only be one path to get us to where we want to be, or that we know the path that God *should* take us through. When we feel as if we aren't going in the optimal route, we don't have the patience to see things through, so instead of holding on, we give ourselves excuses on why we need to jump off the path. Since we don't agree with the path, we make excuses:

- "I wanted to be in the Christmas production, but they chose Sally to be the lead. Anyway, I'm far too busy to get to all of the rehearsals."
- "I know the Bible states that I should tithe to my home church, but why do they need my money? If everyone else tithes, my church is going to be ok."
- "I would host a cell group at home, but James already has the people I would have invited."

Those types of statements always end up with whining, don't they? Why can't Lisa be the lead actor? Why do I have to give the pastor 10%? Why can't James invite his own friends to his cell group? It sounds a lot like what Naaman was saying, "Why can't I jump in the rivers of Damascus, instead?" I'll answer that question for Naaman and then for you. The reason why, Naaman, is that you are the one with leprosy and you came to the prophet of God in Israel to be healed. If you want to go jump in the rivers of Damascus so badly, go ahead and jump in, but you're going to come out with the same leprosy you had when you jumped in. Now, if you want the God of Israel to heal you, I recommend you jump in the water in Israel and only then would He heal you.

The reason why door X is closing on you although you've studied to walk through door X and your heart is set on door X is that behind door X is a path that is going to take you away from your true calling. Door Y has opened for you and somewhere behind door Y is a supernatural force that is going to take you to a level a thousand door Xs could never take you. If you walk through Door Y in faith and confidence in the Lord, His favor will pour out over you and when His favor pours out over you, there is nothing that can stop your ascension. The favor of the Lord can get you places that your resume can't. The favor of the Lord can take you from the lowliest of places and bring you to the highest like he did with young David. The favor of the Lord can take you from a prison cell and living like royalty like he did with Joseph. If you want the true favor of the Lord, simply ask him to open the right doors for you.

When you feel in your spirit that the right doors opened up for you, you need to walk through those doors with the confidence that God is about to make mountains move. When you do that, the favor of the Lord becomes a constant in your life. I'm telling you today to stop avoiding things just because you wish they had been a little different. I spoke with an Associate Pastor who moved to a different city and started working at the church he was led to, but he just couldn't get into it. His old church was, in his words, "full of more fire." His old pastor preached like a preacher, but this new pastor preached like a teacher. His old church had an amazing worship team with talented musicians and anointed singers, but his new church didn't even have a worship team; they would listen to CD's during worship because they were scarce on musical talent. He had left strong ties of brotherhood at his old church and this new church wasn't very warm or inviting.

This friend of mine told me that he thought he was going to die spiritually at this new church, so he sought out another church. He found a much larger church that felt more like his old church. For six months he enjoyed the choir, the music, the preaching and the interaction of the men's group. "Why do I have to jump in those dirty waters of being uncomfortable when I can jump in the waters of Damascus where I'm more accustomed to things?" he said. After a while though, my friend started feeling this emptiness in his spirit. He had a special calling and for six months all he was doing was sitting on a pew. Everything he could think to do was already being done. He prayed to God about it and God reminded him of the church he was led to in the

Your excuse delays your process

first place. It took a while, but he finally realized that God didn't bring him to this new city to sit on a pew at a mega church. He brought him to work side by side with the pastor of that small church!

He went back to that small church and properly introduced himself to the pastor this time and told him that about his experience and qualifications and how he thought he could help this ministry. The Senior Pastor nodded appreciatively and welcomed him to his church. My friend sat there for over a year before he was asked to do anything! "Why jump in the dirty water of Israel" indeed. After a year the pastor asked him to step in and teach the Sunday youth class bi-weekly. Then the other teacher left and he became the weekly youth teacher. After a while the Senior Pastor asked him to put together a men's event. A while after that he transitioned from the youth to be the men's leader. After a while the Senior Pastor told him that there were two couples in church in need of counseling. One marriage was on the verge of a divorce and the other couple was madly in love in need of marriage classes. My friend and his wife started working with those couples.

Later my friend's teenage daughter got pregnant! His experience working with the youth helped him to deal with the situation. Then there was a family clash between brothers. His experience working with the men helped him in that situation. Then his marriage hit a tough patch and their experience working with counseling couples helped them through that situation! My friend never could have coped with what life threw at him had he stayed sitting in a pew at the mega church! It was his experiences and the very words he gave to others that he relied on in his moments of difficulty. Leprosy is a dangerous illness. Your blood flow is thrown off; parts of your body don't get enough oxygen, so they start to spoil and are rendered useless until they just fall off. Your excuse is a form of leprosy because, excuses stop the flow of things, and it slows the process down.

Many lepers where healed instantly, but this leper had to go through a process and his excuses delayed the healing. *Your excuse delays your process.* You are reading this book and it's telling you to stop making excuses for yourself and jump into the water of Israel. Although a spiritual form of leprosy is taking hold of your spirituality, of your finances, of your family life, of your career path, I'm here to tell you that path you need to take might not be the path you are going to like. Common sense will argue with you and tell you that there are cleaner waters out there and you don't need to humble yourself by wallowing in dirty water. I tell you what — if I were Naaman and healing was in that dirty water, I would have jumped in that nasty water as if it were the open ocean.

You might not like where God is leading you, but your job is just to trust in God. It might be a tougher path than you think it should be, but your job is to just trust in God. Some people might look at you a little different because all of a sudden you're putting all of this spiritual content on Facebook, but your job is to trust in God. You may have more qualifications, but if that's the job that God opened up for you, your job is to trust in God. Dip your head in your trust in God and watch the leprosy fall away from your spiritual body. Watch as the weakness of your spiritual self begins to radiate with a new strength.

Chapter 6

The Excuse of "I Can't"

"It's not an excuse; I just can't."

As a disclaimer for this chapter, there are certain things you can't do. You can't decide the price of gas. You can't force everyone in Australia to start speaking Spanish. You can't raise your hands up and fly like Superman. You can't live like an amphibious creature forever. You can't run a mile in five seconds. There are obvious things that you can't do and that is a given. I'm talking about people who use it as a way to stave off conversations without giving good enough reasons. People will use "I can't" as an end-of-conversation weapon. It implies that it is physically out of the person's control and there is nothing he or she can do to change it. *She said she can't, so why keep talking about it?*

However, upon closer examination, we find that "I can't" is not as absolute as people think. The reason people use this excuse is most of the people you talk to are not bold enough to ask, "Well, why not?" If someone does ask, "I can't" is usually followed up with, "I just can't." When you say I *just* can't, it is intended to let the other person know that you have evaluated every option available, but unfortunately there is absolutely no way to do the thing in question. If the conversation would go a little further the real excuse would come out: "I don't have time, my kids are home, I can't afford it," and so on and so forth. The real problem with this is excuse is when you start to believe it.

If you've ever used this excuse, you're in good company. Jeremiah used, it too. The Bible has its share of prophets; some are considered Minor Prophets and others Major Prophets. Jeremiah is a Major Prophet; he even has an entire book dedicated to him! Verses from the book of Jeremiah are one of the most quoted verses today. The book of Jeremiah is a must-read book for all believers. In Jeremiah 1:5 we hear God talking: *"Before I formed you in the womb, I knew you; before you were born I set you apart; I appointed you as a prophet to the nations."* The book begins this dialogue with God, but based on what He is saying, we know that conversations don't just start like this. There is a reason God is saying this to Jeremiah.

Perhaps Jeremiah already threw up an excuse and God was now convincing Jeremiah or maybe Jeremiah had his excuses in his heart, which is why God was saying this. Regardless of whether Jeremiah's hesitation was on the inside or he had expressed it aloud, it is logical to assume that God was laying a foundation of trust with Jeremiah and doing so because Jeremiah needed to hear it. If he needed to hear it that means that for whatever reason, he was refusing, as politely and reverently as possible, to do what the Lord wanted him to do. Since we get access to this conversation after it has already started, it raises some questions. "I appointed you as a prophet to the nations," God told him. Why did God have to tell him this? Because Jeremiah needed convincing!

Maybe you are in this mode as you read this. Maybe you need convincing of something. Search your heart and you'll know what that is. If you're looking for confirmation from someone you know, then you're looking in the wrong place. *"Alas, Sovereign Lord, I do not know how to speak; I am too young" (Jeremiah 1:6).* The word "alas" has finality to it by definition. It's an expression of sadness or unhappiness. Jeremiah isn't asking the Lord to help him. He is stating that he can't do what is being asked of him because he does not know how to speak. Then, in case the excuse of "I can't" doesn't work, his backup is that he's too young. His excuses are so loud to him that they drown out God's voice. His excuses are louder than the very words God Himself spoke over him!

God Himself, the King of Glory, just said told Jeremiah that He knew him even before Jeremiah knew himself. God is telling him, "I know you better than you know you." Then God tells him that Jeremiah didn't choose to be a prophet, God appointed him to be a prophet. I want to take a moment and speak to people in ministry. You didn't decide to go into ministry. It's not like deciding to go to Wal-Mart instead of Target. You were CALLED to ministry. Say that aloud. "I was CALLED BY GOD to be in ministry." Those of you who feel called to get into ministry—the same goes for you. Here's how you can tell the difference: if you're thinking of making money, selling CDs, being famous, having prestige, and/or being well liked—you're *not* being called to ministry. You're forcing your way into ministry. If you want to do the will of God, if you want to serve God by serving others, if your desire is for more people to be saved, if you want to make an impact for the Kingdom of God through any gifts He has bestowed upon you; God is calling you.

God had called Jeremiah into ministry to be His Prophet and Jeremiah had accepted the calling. The problem now was that Jeremiah had to give the people bad news and it scared him to the point where he told God, "I can't!"

Let's park Jeremiah and his self-doubting thoughts here for a few so we can dive into the issue of insecurity. Often the "I can't" stems from not thinking we are good enough, smart enough, eloquent enough, educated enough, polished enough, experienced enough, thin enough, old enough or young enough. These thoughts fester inside of you and build a wall of insecurity that traps you like a prison. It holds you down; it paralyzes you.

If you have felt this way or feel this way now about something I want to tell you that you're ok; it's part of the human experience. We all have moments of insecurity. They are part of our makeup, they creep up on even the most confident, coolest and Godliest of persons. I have wanted to write a book for over 20 years, but at the core of my excuses was my insecurity about my abilities as a writer. Because of my insecurity I lost 276 months, which equates to 1,196 weeks, which equates to 83,395 days. The good thing about belonging to the body of Christ is that you're never alone. God will send help, He will provide shelter, and He will send comfort. In my case, I connected with someone who did know how to write a book and asked for help. That's all you need to do sometimes; ask for help. We live in a world with billions of people, yet some of us allow our insecurities to isolate us and stop us from fulfilling God's promise in our lives. Insecurity stops us from making a bold decision to potentially earn more.

I have a word for you: you may not be able to do something, but if God is calling you to do something—He will bring the resources for you to do it! He opened the Red Sea; He calmed the storm and He infused Samson with strength when he picked up the donkey's jawbone. In Luke 18:35-43 we read the story of Jesus approaching Jericho and how a blind man was sitting by the roadside begging. When he heard the crowd going by, he asked what was happening. They told him, "Jesus of Nazareth is passing by." He called out, "Jesus, Son of David, have mercy on me!" Those who led the way rebuked him and told him to be quiet... just like insecurity does. It tells you that you'll make a fool of yourself. It'll tell you that you're not worth all the trouble.

There are times though when you need to shout past your insecurities. The blind man knew that much. Instead of allowing himself to be shamed into silence, he shouted out louder, "Son of David, have mercy on me!" Jesus stopped and ordered the man to be brought to him. When he came near, Jesus asked him, "What do you want me to do for you?" What a question, right? I tell you what—why don't you answer that question right now? Set this book down for a minute and hear the question Jesus is asking: "What do you want me to do for you?" It was a passionate plea that prompted Jesus to ask him that question. It was a cry for help. There's no shame in a cry for help. I had to reach out to someone who knew how to write a book. My desire was to write this book. It was burning up inside of me; I wasn't confident that I could, but it didn't lessen my desire. It built up inside of me and forced me to cry for help! The Lord put someone in my path who heard my cry.

The Lord asked me, "What do you want me to do for you?"

I answered, "Lord, I want to write a book that has been in my spirit for over 20 years."

The blind man said, "Lord, I want to see."

Jesus said to him, "Receive your sight; your faith has healed you."

Immediately he received his sight and followed Jesus, praising God.

To me Jesus said, "Your faith will be rewarded; you are not alone. Look to your left and your right and you will find one of my children who not only can help you, but wants to help you!" Like the blind man, I saw how to write this book and I'll be forever praising God.

Now let's get back to whiny Jeremiah.

The Lord didn't believe his excuse and guess what? The Lord doesn't believe yours! You can convince the whole world with your excuse, but one day you will have to answer to the Lord as to why you didn't follow the path he set before you. "But the Lord said to me, 'Do not say, "I am too young." You must go to everyone I send you to and say whatever I command you. Do not be afraid of them, for I am with you and will rescue you!'" (Jeremiah 1:7). Whatever your excuse is, the Lord is telling you not to say it. Stop letting those words of defeat and fear come out of His temple. You are a high priest and a temple of the living God. "Go to everyone I send you to and say whatever I command you."

⊷———— *Ex* ————⊷

Because of my insecurity I lost 276 months, which equates to 1,196 weeks, which equates to 83,395 days.

⊷———— *Ex* ————⊷

God laid the smack down on Jeremiah's excuses, just like He does with yours. "Do not be afraid of them, for I am with you and will rescue you." You have to understand that going down the path God is leading you isn't a journey of tranquility. Your spirit will be at peace because you are doing what you are called to do, but expect push back, expect roadblocks, expect trouble. Expect it, but don't fear it. "I am with you and will rescue you," says the Lord. After Jeremiah let go of his securities, the Lord came to him and asked him a question. "And the word of the Lord came to me, saying, 'Jeremiah, what do you see?' And I said, 'I see an almond branch.' Then the Lord said to me, 'You have seen well, for I am watching over my word to perform it.'" What the Lord asked Jeremiah is the same question I'm asking you now. Now that you have gotten past "I can't", what do you see?

PART II

The Solution

Chapter 7

Reasons Versus Excuses —
The Web We Weave

I don't know who said it, but it's been a motto I have consistently quoted throughout my years in the publishing world, "Let's not dwell in the problem, but in the solution." This is the reason I titled the second half of this book *The Solution*. In doing my homework on the subject, I was taken aback and even surprised to find that the word "rationalize" comes from the root word for "reason". This means of course that there's a thin line between a justifiable reason and an outright excuse. It's hard to even write about the topic and it's a lot harder to explain it because we all have our reasons. When we have the right reasons, they protect us and guard us, they propel us to the next step in accomplishing our goals, but here comes the pause in this chapter. How can you tell whether your reasons for not doing something are a bump on the road or really an excuse? My editor sat down with me and wanted me to explain the difference between reasons and excuses, because as I said back in Part I, there are things we that are out of our control. True reasons are important because they help us think correctly. True reasons are not biased; they are tied to truth, but we can still fall down a rabbit hole of using those reasons for too long. That is when they give life to excuses.

Here's a great example: I had to finish a chapter in my book and my editor gave me a deadline (Note to self: all writers need a deadline, if not their book will be like the children of Israel in the desert). She came and hunted me down when I missed the dead-line. I wasn't able to meet it because I had to close out the month with new authors—that was a justifiable reason. It protected me from her wrath and bought me a few more weeks to accomplish my goal. However, here's where fine line between reasons and excuses gets crossed. It became an excuse when I didn't meet the second deadline; even though I got an eye infection and that reason was way better than the first one, the fact remained there still was no chapter. Reasons are important and we all have our reasons—whether it is our faith, our politics, our upbringing or culture. They shape our ideals and correct the course we're walking on, *but* they can become excuses if we always have to explain them. I forgot to add that my pointer and thumb finger got burnt last week while making my old fashion coffee so my reason for being late was physical. However, the reasons quickly became excuses because the list got too long, requiring too many explanations.

Even if your reasons are true, it doesn't make them right. I've had arguments with my wife where she asked me to explain my reasoning and I've said, "I don't have to explain it; I'm just *right!*" Now we know that never works, but we've used statements like, "I said so." That doesn't correct or justify the matter, but in our minds the reason is right and that is our reality, whether it be true or false.

I got a lot of reasons and most are true, but are they right? We need to check our own reality! I wanted to take some time and write this thought provoking chapter because we can easily back up some excuses with true reasons—that still doesn't make it right. We need to look at our reasons and pattern them to our growth; if the reasons are true we need to progress from them. I've had a lot of good reasons for my mistakes and I've inserted excuses to make me feel good about them, but they kept me in the same place of frustration and lack. Take this book and apply the good… I'm sure you may have reasons not to use the whole book, but take what is good for you and *move forward.*

I believe everyone has greatness in them — including you. Whether or not you will live up to the greatness in you depends on where you live a life reasons or excuses. The meaning of these two words is only similar in that they are used to explain something. The problem is that many of us use excuses and try to pass them off as reasons. The problem gets magnified when we actually believe that our excuses are legitimate reasons! Let's take a look at the stark differences between the two.

Reason: A fact, situation, or intention that explains why something happened, why someone did or did not do something, or why something is true.

Excuse: A lie that you give to explain why you have done something or have not done something that you should have done.

The difference between an excuse and a reason is that one is a lie and the other is the truth. Let's say you wanted to go back to school to get a higher level of education or you wanted to take night classes to pick up a new trade. The reason why you didn't would be something like this: The school is too far from me and I don't have a car. Public transportation doesn't go that way and I asked for help from people who live in my area, but they couldn't commit to helping me get there and back three nights a week. Those are valid reasons — they're truth and the truth is that you tried, but it's out of your hands. Here is an excuse: I wanted to go to that school, but I'm so busy already on nights and I work during the day. I need time for me and I'm so busy I couldn't possibly go. That is an excuse; the reason you didn't go to the school is that it wasn't high enough on your list of priorities! Being too busy is one of the most told and believed excuses ever. It's a horrible lie to accept for yourself. If you don't elect to do something because you are "too busy", that means that the other things you did instead are more important to you, so you chose to do those things.

To Live a Better Life You Need To Prioritize!

It's true that we are busy people. We are so busy that even when we are sitting at a bus stop we are doing something on our smart phones. Often we don't start a new venture or embark on a new direction because we are too busy. That doesn't make it right. The ancient Greek aphorism "know thyself" is one of the Delphic maxims and was inscribed in the *pronaos* (forecourt) of the Temple of Apollo at Delphi. This term has lived on for generations because there are so many angles in which it works. Before anything, you need to know yourself. "I'm a child of God." OK… is that it? That can't be it. You truly need to know yourself. Are you a giver of excuses so that you can live a more comfortable life? You need to find out who you are. You are not your nationality, you are not your career, you are not your height and weight, and you are not the name people use to refer to you. Who are you?

Throughout this book you have been asked to make a list or examine yourself and to put things on paper. Have you done it? Is that who you are? Are you the type of person who has the keys to a better life and a better future for your children, but because the elevator is broken, you won't walk up four flights of stairs to find the door? How long will you be that type of person? Here is a quick exercise for you to do to get to know yourself better.

Step 1) Write down the following questions and search your own self for the honest answer:

- How is my spiritual life?
- How is my family life?
- How is my love life?
- How is my financial situation right now?

Step 2) Write down this question for each prior question:

- Why isn't it better?

Step 3) Last question: what do you do with your time instead of working on those four areas of your life?

Step 4) Pick out which ones are excuses and which ones are bona fide reasons. Something has to stir up inside you. You cannot let your life continue on its present course. There is too much at stake here. You have too much to gain.

Is doing what you're doing more important than going to your 6 year old daughter when she calls you?

Is doing what you're doing more important than setting aside 15 minutes to spend with God?

Is doing what you're doing more important than getting a better education?

What in the world are you doing that is so important that you have been stuck in a rut for years?! Are you that selfish that you won't put in the time required to give your family a better life? I know this is sounding a little too harsh, but it's time you hear it. Think on what you did last week and compare it to *what you should have done* last week. Maybe you don't know yourself as well as you thought you did. Perhaps you think you are someone you aren't. Why are you constantly late?

What do you do instead of preparing yourself to leave with enough time to get there even if the traffic is really heavy? This is a super-quick exercise for you to get to know yourself. Make a list of the five most important things in your life and then see how much time you allocate to those things.

Millions of people spend millions of dollars and countless hours learning time management techniques in order to live a more effective daily life. The term "time management", although it appears harmless like most worldly terms, has a subtle hidden mandate that Christians unknowingly follow. When you live your day-to-day life making sure you manage your time well, you will become a master at checking items off of your to-do list. That's not a bad thing. However, you need to believe that God has given you a purpose to live out and a time frame in which to do it in. *Therefore I submit to you that you need to forget time management and instead focus on purpose management!* When you spend your day fulfilling the purpose God has for your life, your day-to-day time will be better spent than managing your time effectively. Your purpose needs to fuel how you spend your time. Otherwise, you will be a task-checking master who has let his or her destiny fall by the wayside! Which person do you think the enemy wants you to be?

"But seek first His kingdom and His righteousness, and all these things will be given to you as well" (Mathew 6:33).

As you have been reading this book, something has been happening to your psyche. A certain level of resolve has started to grow within you, a determination to do more with your life. Some of you know exactly what it is. It is that thing that you know you should have done a long time ago. Now you are ready to set a course that will impact your life. You have noticed time go by and you have stayed the same and you're sick of it. You are angry with yourself for believing the excuses you have been giving yourself and now you are ready to put in that extra effort to better your life. There are others of you who are just as fired up to do something with this new level of resolve that has grown in your belly. The problem is you don't know where to put that energy. You have a full tank of gas and you're at a crossroad, but don't know which direction to go. You are in a good place; don't think you aren't. Having the courage and fortitude to better yourself is half the battle. Unfortunately, I can't tell you what it is you should do. It has to come from you.

We go through life having different purposes at different intervals of our lives. Those of us who know what our purpose is are the ones who live fruitful lives.

Your purpose may not be to open a church and be a pastor, or to start a women's group. Your purpose may be to start a business and to be able to financially sow into the kingdom to help those whose purpose isn't profitable in terms of finances, but profitable to the kingdom of God. We have many purposes in our lives and most of them are different. However, we all share one common purpose and that is to be a blessing to our families. None of us just popped out of the great nothing and started to exist. Find a way to bring about blessing to your family. Don't accept excuses for not doing so. Sow time, forgiveness, joy, laughter, and the attributes of our Lord Jesus Christ into your family. I cannot think of any tasks in your to-do list that should trump that. The excuses that are hindering your life need to be exposed for what they are and they need to be dealt with.

Chapter 8

Some Notes on Fear and Doubt

T here are many factors behind our excuses, but in my years of studying this topic, it mostly comes down to two things: fear and doubt. Fear is the main reason we don't attempt something although that something could provide us with a better life. Doubt is a close second. Fear is "an emotion induced by a perceived threat, which causes entities to quickly pull away from it and usually hide". In short, fear is the ability to recognize danger leading to an urge to confront it or flee from it (also known as the fight-or-flight response), but in extreme cases of fear (horror and terror) a freeze or paralysis response is possible. Fear has also been broken down to mean: False Evidence Appearing Real.

Doubt is a status between belief and disbelief. It involves uncertainty or distrust, lack of sureness of an alleged fact, an action, a motive or a decision. Doubt brings into question some notion of a perceived "reality" and may involve delaying or rejecting relevant action out of concern for mistakes, faults or appropriateness. The reason I wrote this book is I have met far too many people who have been crippled or frozen by fear and or doubt. When I knew them in my childhood or as a young man I, along with everyone else who knew them, thought they had so much potential. Fast-forward to over 20 years later and their potential has shriveled up. They never challenged themselves to be more, to do more. I want better for you!

A quick thought on "potential" while I'm on this topic. Potential is not infinite and it doesn't have the type of shelf life that Twinkies have. Potential expires. If you're a stud high school athlete, you might have the potential to play for a Division 1 college. Once you graduate from high school, the potential has just about evaporated. Three years later, it ceases to exist. If you are in your 30s or 40s, you still have time to reinvent yourself. You have the time to switch careers, learn a new language, learn how to play the guitar, start your own business, sow more time into your children, work on your marriage, etc. However, once you're deep into your 60s, it's too late for so many things. Don't squander your potential! Stop making excuses for yourself and seize the day.

All it takes is heart!

If there were only one person to draw inspiration from in today's time, it would have to be Nick Vujicic (pronounced VOO-yee-cheech). He is an author, musician, actor, and evangelist. However, that may not be why you may have heard of him. Nick has a unique set of limitations. His limitations are justified so much so that he doesn't need excuses for why he can't do something; he has reasons. Nick was born in 1982 in Melbourne, Australia without arms or legs! He never had them, ever. About a year ago I hurt my right thumb very badly and couldn't use it for over a month. Wow, it limited me so much I thought, and that was just my thumb. Can you imagine if I had lost a hand or an arm? I would really have had excuses on why I didn't get to where I wanted to go. Again, Nick was born without any arms or any legs.

The early years of his life were incredibly difficult for him and his family; imagine the amount of time and patience it must take to care for a child like that. Throughout his childhood, Nick had to deal with all of the pressures everyone his age dealt with while in school and going through adolescence. It got to the point where he struggled with despair and loneliness at a level I'm sure not many could comprehend. He continuously wondered what the purpose of his life was, or whether it even had a purpose. However, he found his comfort in the arms of Jesus Christ. A light started to shine from him that people didn't expect. He was actually smiling and engaging with people. In fact, he was so engaging that he had his first speaking engagement at the age of 19. Since then he has traveled around the world. Millions have heard his words, sometimes in stadiums filled to capacity.

He wasn't just speaking to other people with handicaps, but to students, young people, old people, teachers, business professionals, and church congregations of all sizes. He even drives a car! He could have looked at his life and succumbed to despair. If I were a betting man I would wager that people who are constantly giving excuses would not have done what Nick has done if they were in his shoes—that is, if he had shoes. However, Nick understood something that many of us still haven't. It's not about your status, finances, support group or anything else that makes a person successful, it's about the heart. Nick doesn't have arms and hands to grab and take hold of a bright future, but he had the heart.

"If God can use a man without arms and legs to be His hands and feet, then He will certainly use any willing heart!"
—Nick Vujicic

The world is full of people who had every reason to quit or not to achieve what they ultimately achieved. Henry Ford of Ford Automobiles was by all accounts a wealthy man when he began in the automobile industry. Then he went broke. He built himself up and tried again. He went broke again! At that point Henry Ford had a solid excuse to stop trying. Heck, he had given it his all—twice! Still, he failed. Mr. Ford went broke a total of five times before finally succeeding. Colonel Sanders, better known as the founder of Kentucky Fried Chicken, had a nice little restaurant going in the 60s until the construction of a new road put him out of business in 1967. He tried to sell his chicken recipe. The first five people he spoke to didn't buy it. Then he went and pitched it to 20 more; they didn't buy it either. He didn't quit there, though. He mapped out 100 more places to go and sell his recipe, but not one of them bought it.

Imagine being told "no" 100 times. Who would keep going after pitching something 100 times and being told no? How about 500 times? How about 987 times? That is exactly what happened to him. Mr. Sanders ended up going to over 1,000 places before he found a buyer interested in his 11 herbs and spices. He had a mindset that he was going to sell his chicken recipe and that was all there was to it. He didn't give in until he did it. Seven short years later, at the age of 75, good old Colonel Sanders sold his fried chicken company for a finger-lickin' $15 million! Check this out though — he was in his 60s still trying to sell his recipe; he wasn't 25. There are millions of people who have been told that they can't do something and so they quit. The people who do the telling are, for the most part, not experts at it. Most of the time, it's a family member or a good friend.

Fred Astaire went to his first screen test in 1933. The testing director of MGM, someone who supposedly was an expert at showbiz, wrote a memo. Fred Astaire kept that memo over the fireplace in his Beverly Hills home. It said, "Can't act! Slightly bald! Can dance a little!" Here we have an expert telling someone who is trying to get started that he can't do it. In our own lives we have people who are not even experts telling us that we can't do something. If you quit and don't even try, then they were right. Fred is considered one of the best dancers of all time and appeared in 41 films — the guy the testing director for MGM said couldn't act. Have you ever heard of Jimmy Denny? He was the manager of the Grand Ole Opry in 1954. Have you ever heard of someone called Elvis Presley? Well, Mr. Denny fired Elvis after just one performance.

He is most famous for saying these words to "The King of Rock": "You ain't going nowhere son. You ought to go back to drivin' a truck." Somehow I don't think that Elvis quit on himself that day. The truth is that you can find inspiration from your own town; you don't have to get it from people that became famous. There is a bakery store in your town that someone had a dream to open up and he or she did just that. There is someone who speaks three languages that lives near you and just wanted to learn Spanish and German. Wherever you live there are businesses, people losing weight, families forgiving each other. There is a women's group in the near future that will be held near you and someone will be led to know who God is.

Still, it's great to read about people we know, right? OK, I agree, so here are a few more. You may not know the name Rodin, but he sculpted The Thinker statue. His father once said publicly, "I have an idiot for a son." He was considered the worst pupil in school; he failed three times to secure admittance to the school of art. Three times! Our problem is that if we try something once and it fails, we are done trying. He tried four times to get into the school of art he wanted to go to.

"Socrates Nearly Drowns Student"

Imagine that headline. I'm not sure if this is a true story or not, but it is a great story nonetheless. A student asked Socrates for the secret to success. Socrates told the student to follow him and he led him to a nearby river. To the student's surprise, Socrates went into the water and told the student to go with him. When the water got up to their necks, Socrates took the student by surprise and pushed his head under the water.

At first the student, out of respect, wondered why his head was under the water until he needed to breathe. When he tried to get his head out of the water, a surprisingly strong Socrates kept him there until the student started turning blue. The student struggled violently, but Socrates kept his head under the water for an extended period of time. When Socrates let the student up, the boy gasped for air and sucked in deep breaths. "What did you want the most when you were under the water?" Socrates asked. The student replied, "Air." Socrates said, "That is the secret to success. When you want success as badly as you wanted the air, then you will get it. There is no other secret."

What is it that you need? What are you looking for? Do you need motivation? Do you need internal fortitude? I presume that you are a child of the Most High God; what is it that you need? Here are a few more stories that I hope give you what it is you are looking for. Anthony Burgess was 40 when he was told he had a year left to live. He had cancer and it was January of 1960; at that time having the Big C was a certain death sentence. He was completely broke and the thought of not leaving anything behind for his wife troubled him more than the cancerous brain tumor. He had never been a professional novelist in the past, but he always wanted to write and felt he had potential, so he began writing. He didn't even know if his work would be published or whether his wife would get the royalties, but he was short on time so he just wrote and wrote.

He finished five and half novels during that time, but he did not die. His cancer had gone into remission and then disappeared entirely. His books did well though; he is best known for A Clock-Work Orange and wrote more than 70 other books. Many of us are like Mr. Burgess, hiding greatness inside, but only a life-changing emergency would bring it out of us. If you had just a year or two to live, what exactly would you do? Do you see yourself successful? Do you see yourself as great? Do you envision the life you want to live? You should. There is a story about a sales manager who hired sales people, but as a condition of employment, he would take them to the Cadillac dealer and make them buy a new car. The salesman would normally balk at the idea, but for the job, he would buy the car and bring it home.

What do you think the salesperson's wife or husband would say? In the beginning it probably didn't go too well at home for his new salespeople. However, after the spouse would take a ride in the car and drive it around, things would start to change. The neighbors would see them driving in a new Cadillac. People would come over and admire it. Gradually, at a subconscious level, the salesperson's attitude toward his or her own self would change and their earning potential would begin to change. Within weeks they would see themselves as the kind of person who drove a new Cadillac. They saw themselves as big-money earners in their field, one of the top in the industry. Time after time the sales people became superstars. Their sales performance jumped and they earned more than they had ever before; the cost of the new Cadillac wasn't an issue.

It wasn't the fear of making the payment that drove them; it was that they saw themselves as the type of person who drives a new Cadillac. What type of person are you? The type of person you want to be—what things does that type of person do?

Chapter 9

How to Live an Excuse-Free Life

I hope that by now you have come to terms with the fact that the excuses you have used or are still using are doing you harm in many areas of your life. Knowing truly is half of the battle. Unfortunately, just knowing that something is a problem will never get rid of it. You need to install different procedures and processes to effect a change. Don't be afraid of going through a process. Oftentimes God will allow us to go through a tough season or a difficult process because He has something greater in store for us, but at our present state it would do us more harm than good. God says He has plans for us, a plan for good. His plan is not for you to live in poverty, looked down upon by society or to be an afterthought at your job. Living an excuse-free life will take some willpower and dedication, but so does anything worth attaining.

Here are practical tips and steps that you can implement today to get closer to the person you want to become. Some of these have been around for a long time—do you know why? Because they work!

Step 1: Don't be so nice. It's ok to say no!

Some of the times you find yourself giving an excuse are because you didn't have the heart to say "no" to the person or the invite, event, dinner, etc. Simply put, in Mathew 5:37 Jesus tells you to let your "yes be yes and your no be no, anything else is from the evil one." We all know who the evil one is, don't we? He is the Father of Lies. It's ok to say, "No, thank you." If you're too busy, just say you're too busy. If you would rather be home, say that you plan on relaxing at home that day. If you don't have the money just say it. Nothing gets a sales person off your back more than letting him or her know you don't have money! It's better to say no than to commit to something you won't actually do and then look bad.

Simple, yet effective ways to say "no":

- I don't have the time.

- I'm too busy.
- I can't afford that right now.
- My plan for Friday night is to relax at home with the family.
- It's too far away.
- I'm not feeling it.
- No, thank you!

The number one way to get out of making excuses is to not commit to something you don't want to do!

Step 2: Set Goals

I have personally seen the goals that very successful people had written by hand well before they were successful. You need to set two goals, a short-term goal and a long-term goal. Long-term goals can be what you want to do with your life or where you want to be in the next 10 years. Short-term goals are mini targets you need to achieve in order to hit your long-term goals. Immediate goals are things that you can do within the coming two weeks. For example, a long-term goal can be that you want to go to a specific college if you're a high school student. A short-term goal would be to get good grades and get into higher classes. An immediate goal would be to study hard to get an A on the upcoming test.

Long Term Goal: Harvard University

Short Term Goal: Get into higher-level classes and get great grades.

Immediate Term Goal: Study hard to get an A on the upcoming exam.

Now you have a road map on how to best get accepted at Harvard University or any great university. I would strongly recommend that once you have written or typed your goals, share them with someone you trust. The outside pressure that someone else knows that you're slacking at times is all it takes for you to keep pushing through. Also, I recommend that you hang it up somewhere; perhaps in the bathroom so you see it every morning, or refrigerator, or taped to the dashboard of your car.

When setting any goal, you should make sure that it's SMART. SMART stands for Specific, Measurable, Attainable, Relevant and Time-Bound.

Specific — What exactly will you accomplish?

Measurable — How will you (and others) know when you have reached your goal?

Attainable — Is attaining this goal realistic with effort and commitment?

Relevant — Why is this goal important to you? Why does it matter?

Time-Bound — When will you achieve this goal?

Step 3: Have you considered having a Life Coach?

Some of you are just a few steps away from becoming the people you want to be, but don't have the right person holding you accountable for your actions or inactions. At times, your spouse may not be the right person, not even your pastor. Sometimes it can be difficult to tell people who are close to you too much. We feel as if they will look at us differently or that they might not believe in us. I have recently been introduced to the amazing world of Life Coaching. I personally know people who work with Life Coaches and I have seen the dramatic changes. Life Coaching is exactly what it sounds like; they help you manage your life. It's not a nagging wife, a domineering husband or a spiritual father who just tells you to pray about it. A life coach should not be the smartest or most successful friend or relative you have, nor should it be the person you respect the most.

Life Coaching is a profession that is profoundly different from consulting, mentoring, advice, therapy, or counseling. The coaching process addresses specific personal projects, business successes, general conditions and transitions in the client's personal life, relationships or profession. This involves examining what is going on right now, discovering what your obstacles are or what your challenges might be, and helping you choose a course of action to make your life be what you want it to be. Find someone that has gone through a certification process. Life coaching is a profession that requires very specific skills, conduct standards, and a foundation of training, which can only be taught. Life experiences simply are not enough.

FAQs for Life Coaching:

How often do I meet/talk to my Life Coach?

Typically your Life Coach will meet with you every other week at a time that you agree to. Many meetings are in person, but there are also many telephone meetings and online conferencing through programs such as Skype.

How long does Coaching Sessions last?

Typically 60 minutes, but more often they run long. I would not recommend working with a Life Coach who doesn't have 60 minutes per session for you; this is your life we're talking about!

How is Life Coaching different than therapy?

Therapy tends to more about healing, understanding, change, feelings, progress, dealing with past issues and learning to cope with situations. Life Coaching is more about achievement, how to capitalize on momentum, transformation, intuition, performance, and building your life the way you want it.

What type of person hires a Life Coach?

Anyone with a desire to do more and be more. People who understand they need help getting to the next level. The type of people who understand that they would be better if someone could give them instructive advice about their lives, relationships, goals, careers and habits.

Is it expensive?

Define expensive. Most of the coaches I am aware of are very reasonable. I have found Life Coaches to charge anywhere from $40 per hour to $150 per hour. Some of the Christian organizations offer life coaching for donations to their ministry. There are Christian and secular Life Coaches out there. The Navigators Church Discipleship Ministries, Pursuing Promise and others are a good place to start looking.

Step 4: Set Up a Weekly Planner

Now that you have your goals written out and the necessary steps on how to get there, your days need to reflect a life capable of achieving those goals. Your weekly planner should consist of when you wake up and go to bed and everything in between. It should be well balanced with spiritual time, work time, family time and free time. On my Facebook Page you can see a full version of a weekly planner that a writer I know lives by. Take a moment to scan this code and you'll see what I'm referring to. (weekly planner on Facebook page: QR Code) You will find that in this person's schedule he has open times with two different colors. The pink shaded Open Time means he has time, but primarily it is to do something with his wife or family.

The Open Time shaded in beige is where he finds time to watch his recorded TV shows, runs errands, goes to the movies or plays Solitaire. Those open times are also what are used when he is overwhelmed with work so that it doesn't interfere with his family time or his spiritual time. Fill out a weekly schedule of how you lived your life last week. You will be amazed at the time you *waste*. We waste so much time on things that don't get us closer to God, don't get us closer to our family, don't make us better people and don't make us in better shape. Be honest and you might find hours upon hours of TV time and time you just can't account for. Look at your short-term and immediate goals and make time for them appropriately.

Step 5: Get Backup and Get Back Up!

Find someone who you can trust and confide in and let them know what it is you are doing. Beware of the dream killers! My suggestion is that you find a professional Life Coach or even a Mentor from the Navigators who will spend about two hours a month with you; they meet you bi-weekly either in person, over the phone or through a video conferencing service. Most of the Life Coaches I know don't particularly charge a fee directly. They ask for a donation, but it is peanuts for what they do for you. You are the team and you have all the talent, but you may not be a good coach or a General Manager. A well-assembled team (GM) needs great talent (players) to be led by a great leader (Coach) who implements a great strategy (weekly planner and immediate goals) in order to beat the competition (obstacles, excuses) and win the championship (reach your short and long term goals).

Now then, we have a GM, the players, and a coach with a strategy to beat the competition to win the title. Your problem might be that you are the GM, you are also the players (the star player along with the role players), and you are also the coach that doesn't have a winning game plan. *Newsflash* You are not going to win! A Christian-based Life Coach or Mentor will do wonders for you!

Step 6: Set Priorities

Nothing will get you off track like spending time on things you think you should be spending your time on instead of things you really should be spending your time on. Question your priorities. Ask yourself what will get you closer to your goal. Let's get that money making goal out of the way for a moment and let's set some true priorities. These are my personal priorities in their order of importance.

First Priority — Spiritual Life

You don't have to be a pastor and no one is holy, so relax. I'm not saying you have to be perfect. What I am saying is to stay in the race of heaven above all things. Seek first the Kingdom of heaven and all shall follow. This includes cleaning out the guilt, regret, anger, worry, unrealistic expectations, fear and whatever else is keeping you from living a life of love.

Second Priority — Physical Health

When settling in on a plane, a flight attendant will tell you that in the event of a loss of cabin pressure, the gas masks will automatically come out. First put the mask on yourself, then and only then go about and help others if needed. You can't help anyone if you're unconscious! Make sure that you have the right amount of energy to live a fruitful life. You don't need to be a triathlon athlete but a well-balanced life consists of a good diet and time for exercise, even if it's walking the dog.

Third Priority — Family Life

Make sure that you don't forget about your loved ones as you're taking on new challenges. Work on your marriage or it will crumble. Spend time with your kids and talk to them. Take the responsibility of a parent seriously. Either you will teach them about life or someone else will.

Fourth Priority — Sustaining Yourself and Your Family

Be a productive member of society and work. Right now you may not be at the job you love but it's the job you have. It's ok to make plans for a better future, but your current job is paying your current bills and the food you are about to eat so keep working while you are strategizing. Those of us who are married and the other spouse works may have the luxury of taking time off of work to try to accomplish other endeavors, but it should be done responsibly and in agreement.

Fifth Priority — Reach Your Goals

I know you might be wondering why I'm writing a book on getting rid of excuses only to have reaching your goals be last on the list of priorities. If your priorities place your goals ahead of sustaining your family and having a good life with them, taking care of your health and your relationship with God, then your priorities need to be rearranged. Your success may be great if you keep your goals first, but it will also be imbalanced. As much as you succeed with your goals, you will fail in the other areas and no amount of money or business position is worth living that way. In order to help you reach your goals in a healthy way, I have laid out a series of steps that will allow you to do just that if your goals are realistic.

Step 7: Kill It Off!

Nothing inspires someone who is trying to lose weight more than when they lose the first 5-10 pounds.

They may have had doubts on their inner resolve or whether they're on the right diet, but once that weight starts to come off, they settle in for the long haul with confidence. As you accomplish your immediate and short-term goals, check them off. A business owner I know has a list he calls the "Killed It" list. Once he accomplishes a task, he writes it down in the Killed It List. To keep using the analogy of the high school student who wanted to get to Harvard University, this might be a sample of what his or her Killed It List would look like:

Immediate Goals

- Geometry Test – Killed It!
- No missed homework – Killed It!

Short Term Goal

- No lower than a B in Geometry – Killed It!
- Honor Roll – Killed It!

Long Term Goal

- Get accepted at Harvard University – Killed It!

Last, but not least: You must. Stop. Procrastinating. This one is huge! Most of our excuses come from the inability to stop procrastinating. Our procrastination puts us in positions where we need to come up with excuses so that we don't feel foolish. Stop procrastinating. Just stop. How else does it need to be said to you? Procrastination is your enemy. It will hurt you, it will hurt your life, it will hurt your potential and it will kill your dream. There are no brilliant methods that I have seen for someone to follow in order to stop procrastinating. You just have to stop.

Are you upset yet?

You should be. You should be upset at yourself for waiting and waiting and waiting while others bought their homes, went on their vacations, sacrificed a little to get a lot while you're still in the same place as you were before. The types of excuses that you tell yourself are damaging. The ones that hold you back from getting to a higher level—those excuses are poisoning your future. Utilize the tools that you have found in this book. I promise you—they will kill the procrastinator hiding inside of you—but you have to utilize them. Go back and scan those codes. Download the free worksheets. Make your lists and prioritize them. Set SMART goals; write down short and immediate goals as well as how to attain them. Reach out to a Life Coach and find out what that's all about.

Why are you about to turn the page and get to the next chapter? Download the tools and worksheets! It's ok; the book will be right where you left it. I believe a powerful transformation is going to come over you. When you finish doing this legwork, then you can head to the next chapter and see just what your new excuse-free life looks like.

Chapter 10

When You Live an Excuse-Free Life...

————❦————

"No one will be able to stand against you all the days of your life. As I was with Moses, I will be with you; I will never leave you nor forsake you. Have I not commanded you? Be strong and courageous. Do not be afraid; do not be discouraged, for the Lord your God will be with you wherever you go." (Joshua 1:5, 9)

These verses in particular get me fired up. However, it doesn't make me lose my reasoning. Just because I'm fired up to run a marathon doesn't mean I'm ready to run a marathon; it means I'm ready to run a mile and work on my endurance. Too many small businesses have failed because the owner gets fired up and decides to skip steps and just goes out there to "make it happen". Ministry and business are typically powered by different principles. In business, before you engage in running that marathon, you better train or you're not going to make it. You need to prepare yourself and be diligent with the little things. If you're about to open a business, you better do your homework!

Too many Christian business owners think God will bless them to the point that they don't need to try as hard or be as smart. Guess again. If your business model ultimately depends on consumers or clients, you need to know what you're doing, practice moral ethics, work hard and know the landscape of your industry. In ministry, God's favor just takes over at times. This is not to say that God's favor isn't on you in your business, but in ministry God's favor sometimes just doesn't seem fair. Someone can toil for 30 years and pastor a church of less than 100 members, but then another pastor can grow to 500 members in three years. Why? They both serve the same God, don't they? They do. It's just that His favor sometimes just isn't distributed according to our notions of what's fair. If you could talk to Job's first family, I think they would agree. If you could ask Saul, I think he would agree.

God's has a purpose and plan for every life, but His callings aren't all the same. If you are being called into ministry, don't hesitate. Pray that He shows His favor on you and step out in faith. God's goal is that you live with Him eternally. *That's it.* It's not that you will be prosperous and live in a mansion or be on the cover of Forbes Magazine. We need to seek His will in our lives. Once we know His will, we need to go after it. Once we do that and He sees that we can handle it, He gives us more. His will for us increases! Once we have been capable of being faithful in the little, He trusts us to be faithful with more.

Moses

As we read in chapter two, Moses's is story is one of peaks and valleys, moving from miracles to miscues. However, once Moses stopped taking and making excuses, God did absolutely incredible things through him. The Israelites had been slaves for 400 years and here comes Moses marching back into the palace, demanding the Pharaoh to let God's people go. He led a nation through the desert and even brought them to the Promised Land. Even when he made the greatest mistake of disobedience by striking the rock twice, God still honored him in the Mount of Transfiguration. I believe because Moses made excuse in the early stages of his life, but decided to live through them, you will make excuses but you don't have to live by them, they don't have to consume your life and become part of your vocabulary.

Moses's excuse was that he couldn't speak well, but it was Moses that clearly told Pharaoh to let God's people go! See? At the end of the day, when you allow God's will to be done in your life; the very thing that brought fear and doubt to your mind is the very thing that you will conquer!

Chapter 11

God Doesn't Care About Your Excuses

I closed my sermon series by handing out self-made business cards like this one.

I strongly recommend that you download one of these cards available on my Facebook Page. It's free!

Carry it with you—when you feel as if you are starting to give yourself excuses, pull it out and read it. If you feel other people are giving *you* too many excuses, hand it to *them!*

I gave these cards to everyone in the congregation. Even the visitors got one! I challenged them to give the card to the person they you felt was giving them an excuse. Funny stories started to pour into the church as we heard of wives giving husbands the No Excuse card when they were asked to throw out the garbage, a wife being handed the No Excuse card when her husband asked for a foot massage. More than half of the teenagers in the church were handed No Excuse cards from their parents for multiple reasons, but the main reason was not cleaning their rooms. Garages were being cleaned out, bathrooms were being finished, married couples were having a date night, people started saving for long-talked-about and long-overdue vacations and more kids were brushing their teeth!

At first the stories were light-hearted and funny. Then things began to change; people starting taking a closer look at their lives and having the No Excuse card in their wallets was something that they didn't want to give out anymore. The No Excuse card became something that gave them strength, motivation, and determination. Testimonies started to trickle in. Someone got a GED, another person called an estranged brother; someone else opened a business! Life groups popped up, people actually started to come to our Wednesday services, people started inviting their friends to church. There was a shift in our church that was unlike anything I had ever experienced.

We printed out more cards as even non-believers were asking for the card. Then I got a call from a neighboring pastor about the sermon and the cards, and then another pastor from another state called me. My congregation had made a declaration that we were not about making excuses. Those self-defeating prophecies were no longer going to come out of our mouths. It was the best season I ever experienced as a pastor. The legacy of that time still lives today as lives were transformed and new roads were traveled. The transference from negativity to positivity is something that God has bestowed upon me. People tell me when they see me that I'm always smiling. You don't have to know me very well to find out that I don't like to partake in negative talk of any kind. Those who know me well know that I do not allow my kids to speak anything less than greatness over their lives.

I encourage you to do the same. Speak greatness over your life. You need to decide that from this point forward, your past will not hurt your future, and that your financial status will not affect your plans and that your health will not affect your outlook on life and that your reasoning will not cloud what God put in your heart to do. There is a truth about excuses that I hope you can handle. *God doesn't care about your excuses.* He doesn't believe in them. They are of no meaning or significance whatsoever. This world will try to tell you who you are. They will use your finances to tell you who you are or your career, or the language you speak or judge you on your demographic. Unfortunately, some of us have agreed with what the world has to say and our agreement manifests as chronic excuses. Maybe you just need to be reminded of who you are and you will finally see how excuses have held you back.

This is a small sample of who God says you are:

- John 1:12 — You are a child of God.
- John 15:1 — Christ says He is the vine and the Father is the laborer, but that *you* are a branch that will produce much fruit.
- Romans 3:24 — You have been justified and redeemed.
- Romans 8:2 — You are free from the law of sin and death.
- 2 Corinthians 5:21 — You are the righteousness of God.
- Ephesians 1:3 — You have been given *every* blessing from the heavenly realms! The moment you accepted the Lord Jesus Christ as your personal Lord and Savior, you were given every blessing from heaven. God doesn't keep blessings only for those who become leaders in a church, teachers, pastors, evangelists or bishops.
- Ephesians 1:13 — You have been sealed with the Holy Spirit.

- Ephesians 2:10—You were created in Christ Jesus for good works, which God predestined for you.
- Ephesians 5:8—You used to live in darkness, but now you are the light of the Lord.

That is who you are! It doesn't sound like the type of person that gives in easy and cops out with excuses! In Joshua 1 we see the people of Israel in a climactic transition. Moses had just died and Joshua was put in charge. God told Joshua something that every believer needs to understand, as it is meant for us, too. I say it to you now: "During all the days of your life, no one will be able to stand in front of you. As God was with Moses he will be with you. He will not leave you or abandon you. Be strong and courageous." When you live like you truly understand who you really are, you will live an excuse-free life.

Your No Excuses Campaign

For more information on how to establish a No Excuses campaign, please go to my Facebook Page. I have resources for Pastors, Youth Leaders, Worship Leaders, Business Owners, Sales Forces and At Home Moms/Dads. I am launching a National No Excuse Day on February 8, 2015. Many pastors are joining me that day, as well as close friends and family. You can join the movement—we have t-shirts and wristbands! Get your own campaign started and use the #noexcuses hashtag on Facebook, Twitter and Instagram. Join us in this revolution. Let's starve our excuses and feed our destinies!

Acknowledgments

TO THE ONES WHO HELPED SHAPE MY LIFE: To my dad, Reverend Pedro Lopez, Sr.: you are my superhero. I will forever be grateful; your words inspired me to be great in any situation. To my spiritual dad, Reverend Jesus Gonzalez, your example of love and family has sustained me. I also want to acknowledge my mentors and teachers: the pastors Glenn Wilson, Carlos Cádiz, Santo Román, Mizrahim Morales, R.W. Schambach, Joel Lopez, Victor Sanabria, Juan Antonio Sanarina and Ken Hitte.

TO MY BAND OF BROTHERS: Holy Ghost Mission and The Harvest Time Revival Team, #history #revival #legacy: Pastor Ricardo Cortijo, the cream of the crop, Pastor Jose Gabby Mejias—best preacher alive today, Pastor Ruben Tavarez—who can stop you? Norby Torres—The Man! Ariel the Funny Guy and

Richie Dones, you were Paul and we were Timothy. Sound of Praise and Born Twice—love you guys.

TO MY BROTHERS AND SISTERS: Jacob Lopez, the greatest brother one can ever have! Jessie the God Father, Orlando the Truck, Pastor Herson awesomely gifted, Pastor Steve Pound4Pound! The hottest Gonzalez Brother "Soly", my two sisters called Marilyn to Natty and Lisa Please! Julie, Don Brown and to the one I missed the most: my best man Benjamin Nick Gonzalez aka Benji (I can't stop asking why God took you so early, but I do thank him for bringing you to my life). Love you Val

TO MY MOTHERS: Rosa Lopez, I wish I could have been a better son. I love you and miss you so much; I can't wait for my sons to meet you in heaven. To Digna Gonzalez, the greatest mother alive today, the modern-day Mother Teresa, thank you for making me feel so loved every day. To my Titi Awilda: love you mami linda.

THE TEAM OF EDITORS AND WRITING TEAM: Eli "Che" Gonzalez, this book would have taken me a lot longer to finish without you, but it's here today because of you. The world will soon know the gift you have to edit and help write a book. I am happy to have you in my life and can't wait to brand this book with you.

TO THE TEAM AT XULON PRESS: From Chad to Don, Jared, Acquisitions and Production: I can only compare this publishing team to the 1992 Olympic Basketball "Dream Team" or any World Series Yankee team—you guys rock! To the Xulon Press team of editors, sorry for the many commas and misspelled words.

TO MY WIFE AND KIDS: I know I dedicated this book to you, but I want to acknowledge you again. Sorines you are my best friend and the love of my life. My life changed for the better 20 years ago and I will forever be grateful to God for bringing you into my life. To my first born son PJ I love you son you're truly a man and the world can't stop you. To my middle son Jon Jon unguardable in every way gifted and passionate. To Malachi no one has more love then you and you will be great in whatever you choose to do.

TO CHRIST ALONE: You are the source of my life, you are my Rock and My Salvation, everything I have is because of you, I've told you in private and now I'll say it in public. If today were the last day you chose you bless me, I would just say thank you. Your mercy has allowed me to live an awesome life and that's because of you and you alone.

Recommended Readings
by Peter Lopez

Living Beyond the Daily Grind: by Charles R. Swindoll
One of the first books I read and studied. A great friend by the name of Apostle Noel Santiago recommended this book to me 25 years ago and he also ignited a passion for books.

The 21 Irrefutable Laws of Leadership: by John C. Maxwell
It is a complete system about leadership and its John Maxwell teaching about Leadership need I say more.

Paradise Restored: by David Chilton
A great guide to the book of Revelation and the 70 AD Fall of Jerusalem. He was ahead of his time and his book will truly open your mind.

Good To Great: by Jim Collins
I really enjoyed this book which is based on examining companies that made it from decent to really outstanding.

A Tale of Three Kings: by Gene Edwards
The best story telling book and author I've ever read.

Chosen by God: by R. C. Sproul
I read this book 20 years ago and it rocked my world.

Leading on Empty: by Wayne Cordeiro
A MUST read to anyone or everyone in leadership, Could very well be one of the best books written on facing burn out. Do yourself a favor and buy it for you and someone in ministry, they will thank you for it.

Please read and recommend these books
and any other book that touched your life.

About the Author

You know those people who blend in? You meet them and immediately forget their names or see their faces, but you can't remember where.

Peter Lopez is not one of those people.

With a voice to match his big smile, everyone knows Peter because he's pretty much

unforgettable. The thing about Peter is he loves to connect with people and that's one of the many reasons he wrote this book—to connect with you.

With 25 years in business and ministry and now as a Publishing Consultant at Xulon Press, Peter is all about getting to know people. More importantly, his passion is helping them get to know themselves. Whether it's stepping forward in a relationship with

God, a business venture or getting a book published, or being trained and coached, Peter wants to get you moving forward!

Find out more go to his website
www.peterlopezjr.com

15:49

NOTES

NOTES

NOTES

CPSIA information can be obtained at www.ICGtesting.com
Printed in the USA
LVOW05*0903161214

419012LV00005B/46/P